CW00819098

SHIPS IN FOCUS
Anchor and Brocklebank Lines

John Clarkson   Roy Fenton

MANIPUR *1920 as built; see page 46*

Front cover: **TUSCANIA** *1922; see page 15*

Published 1994 by John and Marion Clarkson, 18 Franklands,
Longton, Preston PR4 5PD, United Kingdom.

© 1994 John Clarkson and Roy Fenton

All rights reserved. No part of this publication may be reproduced, stored in a retrieval system or transmitted
in any form or by any means, electronic, mechanical, photocopying, recording or otherwise, without the
written permission of the publisher.

Typeset from disk by Highlight Type Bureau Ltd., Shipley.
Printed by Amadeus Press Ltd., Huddersfield.

ISBN 0 9521179 1 6 [hardback]
ISBN 0 9521179 2 4 [softback]

FOREWORD

How time flies. It doesn't seem like twelve months since I sat down to write the forward to our first book, *Ships in Focus: Ellerman Lines*. At the time, we were hoping that a combination of good, well-reproduced photographs and informative captions would make for a successful book. We seem to have been right - as other publishers have noted - so here goes with number two.

We felt the subject of the next book should be one about which little has been written, or few photographs published. As this is a series of "photographic albums" - as some have referred to *Ellerman Lines* - it is most important that we put together a good selection of photographs. Looking through the Feilden Collection, Anchor and Brocklebank Lines appeared possibles but neither would make a book on its own. But were they connected? Browsing through a Lloyds Loading List from the twenties the answer was found. The two companies ran joint services for several years, as evidenced by the advertisement reproduced on page 35, and research showed there were also financial connections.

As with *Ellerman Lines*, most of the photographs have come from collections which I hold, mainly those of Feilden and McRoberts, but there were gaps which needed to be filled. Keith Byass, Cliff Parsons, Tony Smith and Harry Spong filled in some of these from the collections held by the World Ship Society. Malcolm Cranfield and Vic Young, long-standing friends, helped with some more recent Brocklebank vessels. Ian Spashett of Fotoflite also supplied some photographs, as did Alec Duncan. The main gaps then left to be filled were the tenders owned by Anchor Line, and the notable motor coaster FULLAGAR, owned by Brocklebank for a short time. A picture of the latter was tracked down to the Williamson Art Gallery and Museum at Birkenhead, whilst Donald Robertson, in collaboration with Graham Langmuir, provided some of the tenders. To all of them, and to others not mentioned above, but not forgotten, go our grateful thanks: their work is acknowledged after the caption to their photograph. Thank you also to everyone for their encouragement and support and to those involved in all stages of the production of this book.

John Clarkson, Longton, June 1994

In the captions I have attempted to describe the ship's place in history and give an outline of her career. Gross tonnages quoted are those when bought or built, and lengths are usually overall. A list of sources follows the Brocklebank history on page 36, but I must make special mention of my friend Captain Ken Garrett to whom I owe a big debt for sharing memories of the Brocklebank ships on which he served.

Roy Fenton, Wimbledon, June 1994

CALIFORNIA (3) *Alexander Stephen & Sons Ltd., Linthouse; 1923, 16792 gt, 553 feet*

Anchor Lines' CALIFORNIA was essentially a North Atlantic ship but each year made several sailings to Bombay. She was taken over for conversion to an armed merchant cruiser in 1939, and served in this role until April 1942. By then there was a need for troopships and in this capacity she made two voyages to both South Africa and India. Her third trooping voyage was her last, and en route to Freetown she was bombed and set on fire by aircraft west of Portugal on 11th July 1943.

ANCHOR LINE - AN ENDURING NAME

A title which embodied the Victorian virtues of permanence and dependability ensured that, in name at least, Anchor Line has survived for almost 140 years. Its independent existence, however, spanned less than half this period.

Anchor Line is generally regarded as dating from 1856, when a steamship service was inaugurated between Glasgow and New York by the Handyside Brothers and Thomas Henderson, a partnership which already ran sailing ships in a number of trades. Anchor's early North Atlantic services were decidedly patchy: the ships were undistinguished, there were several losses and steamers were transferred to other trades when profitable opportunities presented. Ships were also diverted as services from both Scotland and North America to the Mediterranean were introduced. It was not until the 1870s that the business was well enough established to attract its first - albeit unsuccessful - take-over bid, from the Pennsylvania Railroad Company.

The retirement of the last Handyside in 1873 encouraged the Henderson family to expand its empire, taking an interest in the Tod and MacGregor shipyard at Partick which, as D. and W. Henderson, was to build many Anchor Line ships. Another sign of the family's growing confidence was their substantial stake in the Barrow Steam Ship Company, formed in 1872 as part of an attempt to stimulate the growth of Barrow as a transatlantic port and centre for shipbuilding. The former did not materialise, but a number of ships built at Barrow for the new company were used on Anchor Line routes. The decade also saw what was to be Anchor's other major route established, with services from Glasgow and Liverpool to Bombay beginning in 1875.

The deaths of the four senior members of the Henderson family within three years in the 1890s brought to a close Anchor Line's years of growth. Following a change of name to Anchor Line (Henderson Brothers) Ltd. in 1899 there was a period of consolidation in which the fleet came to include fewer, but larger and more specialised ships for its North Atlantic and Indian routes, the U.K. to the Mediterranean service having been discontinued in the 1890s. This was the first formal use of Anchor Line as part of the title of a shipowning company: previous ships had been owned or managed under the names of various Hendersons.

The company's independence ended in 1911 when its shares were bought by the Cunard Steamship Co. Ltd., which already had a strong base in the North Atlantic trades. There were to be far-reaching consequences for Anchor Line, but the only outward change was the addition of a white line between the black hull and red boot topping, which added considerably to the ships' smartness. In 1912 Anchor's Calcutta services were transferred to Brocklebanks, the ships being repainted in the latter's colour but retaining their names. The service was given the title Anchor Brocklebank Line. A further joint operation imposed by the new masters was Anchor-

Donaldson Ltd., established in 1916. Four Donaldson Line ships were transferred to this company to operate a service between Glasgow and Eastern Canada.

Anchor Line passenger ships suffered harshly during the First World War, and only the COLUMBIA survived. Resuming peacetime sailings to New York therefore necessitated diverting ships from Indian services. The post-war reconstruction programme was ambitious, involving five new ships bigger than any previous Anchor Line vessels. Alas, circumstances did not justify such an investment, with recession and the drastic reduction in emigration to North America in the 1920s ending the service from the Mediterranean to New York. Even though completion of some vessels was postponed Anchor Line had surplus tonnage which it found difficult to employ fully. The result of this and the generally depressed trading conditions was that by the 1930s the company was in financial difficulties, as indeed was its parent. In 1935 Anchor Line (Henderson Brothers) Ltd. was liquidated and its assets transferred to Anchor Line (1935) Ltd. in which Runciman (London) Ltd. had a major stake. New ownership brought a fresh injection of capital which allowed new passenger ships to be ordered for the Indian services.

Once again war hit the company's ships hard. Only one of the Atlantic passenger liners remained in 1945, and the replacements were cargo liners with very limited passenger accommodation. As a result, the Bombay service assumed a new importance to Anchor Line. Behind the scenes, ownership was changing again, with the United Molasses Co. Ltd. acquiring a majority of the share capital between 1949 and 1953. Both the effect and duration of this ownership was limited, and in 1965 Runcimans re-acquired their majority interest. The 1960s saw the end of much of the company's traditional trade. Passenger sailings to India ceased early in 1966. Even though fine new cargo liners were built for the North Atlantic, the rapid growth of containerisation made them redundant and this service closed in 1967. But again, possibly because of its hallowed name, Anchor Line continued with renewed vigour. Runciman's operations were transferred from Newcastle to Glasgow, whilst Moor Line ships were registered under Anchor Line ownership and took the remaining sailings to India. Large and sophisticated bulk carriers were ordered. And as parent company Walter Runciman plc bought other Scottish companies in the early 1970s, their ships were registered under Anchor Line ownership in the case of George Gibson and Co. Ltd. or managed from its office in the case of Currie Line Ltd. The latter's small dry cargo ships were soon sold, but the gas carrying business has continued, and in 1994 a small fleet of tankers remains under the ownership of Anchor Line Ltd. Anchor Line was perhaps Glasgow's best known shipping company, and its name has meant that it has endured to be one of the city's last.

BARROW STEAMERS

ANCHORIA (1)
Barrow Shipbuilding Co., Barrow; 1875, 4168gt, 408 feet

Amongst the earliest Anchor Line vessels photographed were the three near-sisters shown on this page. Remarkably, they each carried one thousand passengers, mostly in steerage. Despite her name, ANCHORIA was built for the Barrow Steamship Co. Ltd. and not transferred to Henderson Brothers ownership until 1893. Tripling her engines in 1887 extended her life, and she traded until 1906 when she was sold to Germany for use as an accommodation hulk, as which she served until well after the First World War.

DEVONIA
Barrow Shipbuilding Co., Barrow; 1877, 4270gt, 400 feet

DEVONIA was also owned by the Barrow Steamship Co. Ltd., managed by Henderson Brothers and operated on Anchor Line services. She had a relatively short active life, her regular Anchor Line sailings finishing in 1893. Thereafter she spent much of her time laid up until being sold to Hamburg breakers in 1899. Although in this view DEVONIA crosses fewer yards than the ANCHORIA, the white canvas of her furled sails can be clearly seen.

CIRCASSIA (1)
Barrow Shipbuilding Co., Barrow; 1878, 4272gt, 400 feet

The third of the Barrow trio was notable as being the first North Atlantic refrigerator ship, with capacity for about 400 carcasses of frozen beef. Her career on the Glasgow to New York route paralleled that of DEVONIA, and after finishing regular sailings in 1897 she was broken up in Hamburg during 1900.

HENDERSON-BUILT

BRITANNIA (2)
D. & W. Henderson & Co., Partick; 1879, 3069gt, 350 feet

In 1873 a Clydeside shipyard was acquired by members of the Henderson family, including the partners in Anchor Line. Under the title D. & W. Henderson & Co., this yard built many ships for the line, second of which was the BRITANNIA. Given a new engine in 1895, she lasted until 1909, when she was sold to Bombay owners and broken up almost immediately.

KARAMANIA
D. & W. Henderson & Co., Partick; 1883, 3148gt, 340 feet

During Anchor Line's years of rapid expansion during the last quarter of the nineteenth century, ships were often moved from one service to another. KARAMANIA began life on Indian routes but during her career was also employed on services between the Mediterranean and New York. She was delivered to the Barrow Steamship Co. Ltd. and operated by Anchor Line; Henderson Brothers formally acquiring her in 1893. She was broken up in 1904.

ARABIA
D. & W. Henderson & Co., Partick; 1884, 3344gt, 378 feet

ARABIA was one of four sisters built for the Indian services, but along with other Anchor Line ships shown on this page she had a large capacity for steerage passengers, which suggests a design intended to be suitable for North Atlantic services. ARABIA was sold to Italy in 1908 and subsequently demolished.

PASSENGER SHIPS FROM BARROW

CITY OF ROME
Barrow Shipbuilding Co. Ltd., Barrow; 1881, 8415gt, 560 feet

With her clipper bow, three funnels, four masts and apparently enormous length, CITY OF ROME was one of the most striking Atlantic liners of her day, but her performance did not match up to her looks. She was ordered by Inman Line but failed to reach her contract speed and was returned to her builders. Transferred to the associated Barrow Steam Ship Co. Ltd., she was operated by Anchor Line initially between Liverpool and New York. She became a popular ship, but was not to be a long-lived one and, outmoded by the pace of development on the Atlantic, was broken up in Germany early in 1903.

FURNESSIA
Barrow Shipbuilding Co. Ltd., Barrow; 1880, 5495gt, 445 feet

Fourth of the Barrow ships running from the Clyde to New York was the FURNESSIA, a size larger than her companions shown on page 4 and distinguished by two funnels. As shown in the lower photograph, these were replaced with one when her engines were tripled in 1891, although she retained her yards for some years. FURNESSIA was officially acquired by Henderson Brothers in 1893 and sailed on, latterly with only second and third class accommodation. In 1911 she was stripped at Barrow and arrived at Preston early the next year to be broken up by T.W. Ward Ltd.   *[Lower: W. Robertson & Co.]*

COLUMBIA (2)
D. & W. Henderson & Co. Ltd., Partick; 1902, 8292gt, 485 feet.

COLUMBIA was a replacement for the CITY OF ROME, although she was much the same size and no faster. Her career was to be much more varied, however. During the First World War she served on the Northern Patrol as the armed merchant cruiser H.M.S. COLUMBELLA, being the only one of Anchor's major passenger ships to survive. With the arrival of larger and more modern tonnage, she was sold in 1926 to Greek owners as MOREAS, although initially retaining British registry. Her service between Piraeus and New York was patchy, and she was broken up at Venice in 1929.

CALEDONIA (3)
D. & W. Henderson & Co. Ltd., Partick; 1904, 9223gt, 500 feet

A replacement for the ANCHORIA of 1875, the splendid-looking CALEDONIA could accommodate almost fifteen hundred passengers. This made her an ideal candidate for trooping, and she was requisitioned immediately on the outbreak of the First World War.

CALEDONIA was in the Mediterranean bound for Malta and a refit in December 1916 when attacked and sunk by U 65. Although the merchant ship was regarded as a legitimate target for the submarine, the Germans did not consider the reverse to be the case, and the attempt made by CALEDONIA's master to ram U 65 resulted in his facing the same fate as Captain Fryatt of the cross-channel steamer BRUSSELS: trial followed by summary execution. Following threats delivered to Germany through diplomatic channels, CALEDONIA's captain was spared and sent to a prisoner-of-war camp.

CALIFORNIA (2)
D. & W. Henderson & Co. Ltd., Partick; 1907, 8662gt, 470 feet

The outbreak of the First World War found the CALIFORNIA hard aground on Tory Island, off the north of Ireland. This may have spared her from Government requisition, as after prolonged salvage and repair she resumed sailings between Glasgow and New York late in 1915. It did not save her from submarines, however, and on 7th February 1917 U 85 torpedoed her south west of Fastnet with the loss of 43 lives.

CAMERONIA (1)
D. & W. Henderson & Co. Ltd., Partick; 1911, 10963gt, 515 feet

During the First World War CAMERONIA was left running on the North Atlantic until January 1917 when taken over for trooping. This service was to be tragically short. On 15th April 1917, two days out from Marseilles on her second voyage to the eastern Mediterranean, she was torpedoed by U 33 and sank with the loss of 229 from the 2,650 on board.

TRANSYLVANIA (1)
Scott's Shipbuilding & Engineering Co. Ltd., Greenock; 1914, 14315gt, 548 feet

TRANSYLVANIA was ordered for a joint Anchor-Cunard Mediterranean service, but with the outbreak of war she was diverted to Cunard's North Atlantic route. Anchor Line bought her for their own New York service in 1915, but she was quickly requisitioned for trooping.

She was the third of Anchor's major passenger ships lost within a few months. On 4th May 1917 she was on a voyage from Marseilles to Alexandria when, despite her escort of two Japanese destroyers and her constant zigzagging, she was sunk in a determined torpedo attack by U 63. Over 400 of her complement of more than 3,000 were lost.

OLYMPIA (2)
D. & W. Henderson & Co. Ltd., Partick; 1902, 5124gt, 400 feet.

OLYMPIA and her near-sister MASSILIA were essentially cargo ships for the Indian service with accommodation for just over 50 cabin-class passengers. However, such was Anchor Line's shortage of ships following the First World War that both were diverted to the North Atlantic service at various times. After returning to the Bombay route, OLYMPIA was broken up at Ardrossan in 1926.

CIRCASSIA (2)
D. & W. Henderson & Co. Ltd., Partick; 1902, 6717gt, 450 feet

CIRCASSIA was notable for spending her entire career running to India, even when requisitioned by the Government during the First World War. She is seen off Birkenhead Docks late in her career, which ended at the breakers in 1931.

CASTALIA (2)
Barclay, Curle & Co. Ltd., Whiteinch; 1906, 6388gt, 441 feet

Although Anchor Line's association with D. & W. Henderson's yard ended in 1899, only slowly did the line turn to other builders such as Barclay, Curle. Their CASTALIA survived both wars, and in 1949 could still find buyers in the shape of Italians running services to Central America. After five years running as MARENGO and URANIA II the old ship was broken up in Japan at the end of 1953.

ELYSIA (2)
D. & W. Henderson & Co. Ltd., Partick; 1908, 6368gt, 441 feet

During the First World War ELYSIA had torpedoes fired at her at least five times, the last attack in May 1918 causing heavy casualties and severe damage. She showed a similar capacity to take punishment during the Second World War. After an attack by a group of Japanese surface raiders and submarines in the Indian Ocean on 5th June 1942, it took several torpedoes and four days before ELYSIA sank.

TARANTIA (1)
Russell & Co., Port Glasgow; 1911, 4754gt, 400 feet

Although by 1915 Anchor had not lost any ships to enemy action, several had been requisitioned by the Government. Replacements included the Glasgow-owned cargo steamer KIRKFIELD, which was renamed TARANTIA. She served Anchor well, and was not sold until 1937 when she became the Greek LEONTIOS TERYAZOS. In June 1940 she fell into German hands at Bordeaux and was renamed RASTENBURG, as which she was scuttled in the Gironde in August 1944.

VITELLIA
Earles' Shipbuilding & Engineering Co. Ltd., Hull; 1918, 4449gt, 376 feet

In 1919 Cunard bought two B-type war standard ships from the Shipping Controller for the company's North Atlantic cargo service: VITELLIA, ex-WAR PINTAIL, seen here and VINDELIA. Both were almost immediately transferred to Anchor Line ownership, but in 1924 were sold to the Scindia Steam Navigation Co. Ltd. of Bombay, the VITELLIA becoming JALARASHMI. She worked under Indian ownership for 30 years, after which she was worn out. Indeed, the crew taking her from Bombay to the breakers as ASHA refused to go further than Singapore, and she had to be towed from there to Japan as ASHA MARU. She was broken up in June 1955.

EXPRESS
D. and W. Henderson & Co., Partick; 1880, 272gt, 150 feet
Over the years Anchor Line used several tenders and tugs to serve their ships on the Clyde and in Lough Foyle. First of these was the twin-screw EXPRESS, whose large crane would have been useful for swinging passengers' luggage ashore. After 33 year's service she was sold to T.W. Ward Ltd. and arrived at Preston for breaking up in April 1913. *[D. Robertson & G.E. Langmuir]*

PALADIN
Murdoch & Murray Ltd., Port Glasgow; 1913, 366gt, 140 feet

PALADIN was a replacement for the EXPRESS. One of her moments of glory came when attending the QUEEN MARY during her first sailing from the Clyde in 1936. PALADIN's connection with Cunard continued when sold to this company in 1939, and she continued in use on the Solent until 1961, latterly under Red Funnel ownership.

SEAMORE *J. P. Rennoldson & Son, South Shields; 1891, 262gt, 132 feet*

In 1928 Anchor Line bought for use on Lough Foyle the old paddler AMERICA, which had begun life under the ownership of the Clyde Shipping Co. Ltd. She returned to the Clyde during the Second World War to attend the many extra ships using the river, a service which left her tired out. The only available photograph of SEAMORE shows her awaiting the breakers' torch at Port Glasgow in April 1946, and is made more interesting by the presence of the Manx steamer SNAEFELL. Built in 1907, she too had seen hard war service maintaining sailings for the Isle of Man Steam Packet Co. Ltd., and was also laid up in 1945 to await demolition.

[D. Robertson & G.E. Langmuir]

CYNTHIA
J. T. Eltringham & Co., South Shields; 1892, 272gt, 153 feet.

The paddler CYNTHIA seems to have begun life as a tug and tender, and later to have been elevated in status to an excursion steamer. She was bought by the Moville Steam Ship Co. Ltd. in 1907 and used as tug, as a tender for Anchor and Allan Line ships calling at Lough Foyle, and for pleasure cruises out of Londonderry, as seen here. Anchor Line acquired her on the demise of the former owners in 1928. Sold to Belfast operators in 1931, she was wrecked at Dun Laoghaire two years later.

[D. Robertson & G.E. Langmuir]

CAMERONIA (2)
William Beardmore & Co. Ltd., Dalmuir, 1920; 16280gt, 575 feet

CAMERONIA was the first of Anchor Line's much-needed post-war ships for the North Atlantic. She was launched in record time but her entry into service was delayed by an industrial dispute over the ending of bonus payments, and she had to be taken to Cherbourg for completion. Her career was long and varied, and as a Second World War troopship she was involved in the invasions of North Africa, Sicily and Normandy. This left her apparently worn out, but CAMERONIA was brought out of lay-up in 1947 for further trooping and later carrying emigrants to Australia. Her story continues on page 34.

ASSYRIA (3)
A.G. Friedrich Krupp Germaniawerft, Kiel, Germany; 1908, 8142gt, 448 feet

Anchor Line bought just two ex-German ships after the First World War, including ASSYRIA which had been built for Hamburg Amerika as YPIRANGA. The cargo-passenger ship was intended for the Bombay route, but after entering service in 1921 she spent four years running to New York, such was the shortage of North Atlantic ships. Sold in 1929, she enjoyed a long career serving Portugese colonies as COLONIAL, lasting until 1950 when she was wrecked off Scotland, heading to Clydeside breakers as BISCO 9.

TUSCANIA (2) *(top)*, **NEA HELLAS** *(middle)* **and NEW YORK** *(bottom)*
Fairfield Shipbuilding & Engineering Co. Ltd., Govan; 1922, 16991gt, 552 feet

As her name suggests, the splendid TUSCANIA was intended to trade between Italy and New York, but the imposition of U.S. immigration quotas meant she made only a few such voyages. TUSCANIA was then used on a number of Anchor and Cunard services, including Anchor's routes from the U.K. to New York and to Bombay, Cunard's London to New York service, plus a certain amount of cruising and trooping.

In 1939 she was sold to the General Steam Navigation Co. Ltd. of Greece and became NEA HELLAS, but with the fall of Greece she returned to British control and Anchor Line management. After a war spent trooping her Greek owners refitted her for their Mediterranean to New York service: she is seen here at Naples. After a further refurbishment she was renamed NEW YORK in 1955, and steamed on until 1961 when broken up in Japan.

[Middle: E. Johnson]

TRANSYLVANIA (2)
Fairfield Shipbuilding & Engineering Co. Ltd., Govan; 1925, 16923gt, 552 feet

Perhaps believing that passengers still equated number of funnels with power and speed, Anchor Line put three on ships which were no larger and only a little more powerful than the TUSCANIA. Construction of TRANSYLVANIA was begun in 1923, but she lay on the stocks incomplete for some time before being delivered in September 1925. Her service was largely on the Glasgow to New York route, with a little cruising from New York to the West Indies in the late 1930s. Duty as an armed merchant cruiser during the Second World War was terminated when she was torpedoed by U 56 on 10th August 1940 whilst off Ireland, outward bound from Glasgow to patrol the North Atlantic.

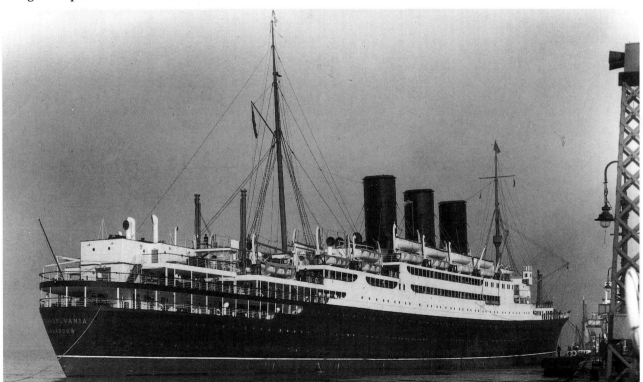

CALEDONIA (4)
Fairfield Shipbuilding & Engineering Co. Ltd., Govan; 1925, 17046gt, 553 feet

Sister to the TRANSYLVANIA, the CALEDONIA had a similar life and death. Although laid down ahead of her sister, she was completed slightly later, to become the fourth of the ships that sustained Anchor's North Atlantic services between the wars. In parallel with the TRANSYLVANIA, she became an armed merchant cruiser in September 1939, taking the name H.M.S. SCOTSTOUN. She too fell victim to a German submarine west of Ireland whilst serving on the Northern Patrol. The culprit was U 25, and the date 13th June 1940.

BRITANNIA (3)
Alexander Stephen & Sons Ltd., Linthouse; 1926, 8464gt, 460 feet.

BRITANNIA was the only cargo-passenger vessel which Anchor Line built for their Indian services in the years immediately following the First World War. The line suffered particularly badly in the Second World War, and the BRITANNIA was intercepted by the German raider THOR 750 miles west of Freetown on 25th March 1941. Her adversary was formidably armed with 5.9 inch guns and torpedo tubes, and BRITANNIA sank with heavy casualties: 249 out of the 492 crew and passengers aboard.

CIRCASSIA (3)

Fairfield Shipbuilding & Engineering Co. Ltd., Govan; 1937, 11136gt, 484 feet

With fresh capital available following the take-over by Runciman, Anchor Line began to invest in new tonnage for their Indian services. For their first diesel-powered liners they returned to Fairfields who had built their last North Atlantic vessels. The ships were good investments, and saw out the Indian services; CIRCASSIA - the first delivered - taking the last passenger sailing from Glasgow and Liverpool to Bombay in January 1966, after which she was broken up in Spain.

CILICIA
Fairfield Shipbuilding & Engineering Co. Ltd., Govan; 1937, 11136gt, 484 feet

CILICIA's Anchor Line career closely paralleled that of CIRCASSIA: war service first as an armed merchant cruiser and later as a troopship, followed by almost two decades on the Bombay route. When this was due to close late in 1965 she was found a new role as a hostel for dock workers in the port of Rotterdam, where as JAN BACKX she became a familiar sight moored beneath the Euromast. This sedentary role extended her life until 1980, when she was scrapped in Spain.

CALEDONIA (5)
Fairfield Shipbuilding & Engineering Co. Ltd., Govan; 1948, 11252gt, 484 feet

Heavy war losses necessitated further passenger tonnage for the Indian services, but the uncertainty caused by India's forthcoming independence led Anchor to take the modest step of ordering a third ship to the pre-war design. CALEDONIA's career as a liner was cut short by the ending of the Indian service in 1965, but she found stationary employment as a student hostel in Amsterdam until 1970 when she went to Hamburg for scrap.

TARANTIA (2)
William Doxford and Sons Ltd., Sunderland; 1942, 7268gt, 429 feet

Its war losses entitled Anchor Line to build ships to its own account during the Second World War. Two fairly basic Doxford motorships were delivered in 1942, but only the TARANTIA survived the war. She was sold out of the Anchor fleet in 1959, becoming first the Greek CAPE VAMVAKAS and later the Cypriot BUONAVIA, as which she was broken up in China during 1971.

TAHSINIA (2)
Lithgows Ltd., Port Glasgow; 1946, 5680gt, 433 feet

TAHSINIA was a post-war replacement for a short-lived Doxford motorship of the same name. Transferred from the Indian to the North Atlantic services in 1956, her modest 12 knots was inadequate and in 1959 she was sold. As CARACAS and AGIOS THERAPON she tramped for ten years for New York and Greek owners respectively, finally arriving at Shanghai for demolition as the Greek PARALOS late in 1969.

TYRIA (top), KING JAJA (middle) and ESPEROS (bottom)

William Doxford and Sons Ltd., Sunderland; 1955, 5869gt, 451 feet

Although built ten years after the war, the TYRIA was essentially a modernised version of the war-built TARANTIA, with better accommodation and cargo gear, but no greater speed. Although quickly transferred from the Indian to the North Atlantic service, she was outclassed and was sold after only four years with Anchor Line. Later owners got better value from her; first Nigerian National Line for whom she ran as KING JAJA from 1959 to 1975, and her final Greek owners for whom she traded under the Cyprus flag as ESPEROS until broken up at Gadani Beach in 1978. The photograph of ESPEROS was taken soon after renaming at Liverpool in November 1975.

[top: World Ship Photo Library]

EGIDIA (1) *(top)* **and BENHOPE** *(bottom)*
Lithgows Ltd., Port Glasgow; 1945, 9942gt, 476 feet

With three of Anchor Line's North Atlantic liners having become war casualties, the decision was taken to buy standard, war-designed, cargo liners with limited passenger accommodation to reopen the services. These motorships served on the North Atlantic until they replaced the "T" class ships on the Indian services. EGIDIA found a British buyer in the shape of Ben Line when made redundant by Anchor in 1962, and as BENHOPE sailed on for another ten years until broken up in Taiwan.

ELYSIA (3)
Lithgows Ltd., Port Glasgow; 1945, 9979gt, 476 feet

Second of the war-designed group, ELYSIA served Anchor until 1963. After a spell under the Liberian flag as ATHENIAN she returned to British - or rather Hong Kong - ownership as Swire's NINGHAI in 1966. Returning to a flag-of-convenience she became the Panamanian VENUS NINGHAI in 1971 and was broken up in Taiwan two years later.

EUCADIA (1) *Barclay, Curle & Co. Ltd., Whiteinch; 1945; 7005gt, 476 feet*

Of the three "E"s, only EUCADIA came to a violent end. Anchor sold her in 1963 to Frangos Brothers who renamed her IONIAN and almost immediately MACEDON. In November 1964 she went aground and broke up at Ras Beirut during a voyage from Houston to Bombay.

SIDONIA *(top)* **and HUPEH** *(bottom)*

C. van der Giessen en Zonen's Scheepswerven N.V., Krimpen a/d Yssel, Netherlands; 1961, 5705gt, 473 feet
To modernise the Anchor fleet, three fast cargo liners were built in the 1960s. Considered somewhat avant garde at the time, the engines three-quarters aft design has stood the test of time well. SIDONIA caused something of a stir as she was built by a Dutch rather than a Scottish yard. Her North Atlantic career was rather short, and in 1967 she went to Swire's China Navigation Co. Ltd. as HUPEH. The lower photograph shows her under this name in charterer's funnel colours, after Swires had converted her to a side-loader. She was later to become a partial container ship. The inevitable flag-of-convenience owners claimed her in 1982 and as SUN OPAL and NEW UNITED she worked until meeting her end in Kaohsiung's scrap yards in 1985.

[top: Fotoflite incorporating Skyfotos]

ELYSIA (4)

Hawthorn, Leslie (Ship Builders) Ltd., Newcastle; 1965, 6499gt, 486 feet

British, if not Clydeside, yards got the belated orders for SIDONIA's larger running mates, beginning with ELYSIA, which was officially owned by Athel Line Ltd. The photograph was taken in September 1967, very shortly before she too went to other owners. For Strick Line Ltd. she ran to the Persian Gulf as ARMANISTAN, in 1975 becoming STRATHAVOCH in accordance with parent company P & O's dictates on corporate identity. Her last years from 1978 were spent as the Hong Kong-owned SHARP ISLAND until Taiwan breakers took her in 1983.

ANAT ex-SICILIA

Bartram & Sons Ltd., Sunderland; 1965, 6120gt, 470 feet

SICILIA was the last of the new cargo liners built for the joint Anchor-Cunard services, and emerged just in time to see the North Atlantic routes containerised. Sold in 1968, she became the ANAT as seen here, eventually finding her way to the ownership of Zim Israel Navigation Co. Ltd. of Haifa. In 1974 she passed to the parent company, Shoham Maritime Services Ltd., as the Liberian-flag GOLD STAR. Five years later she became the Greek GOLEMI before the Gadani Beach breakers claimed her in 1986.

EUCADIA (2)
Hawthorn, Leslie (Ship Builders) Ltd., Newcastle; 1961, 5924gt, 468 feet

In 1965 Anchor Line was sold back to Walter Runciman and Co., and a degree of rationalisation of the two company's shipping interests followed. The result was an apparent reverse take-over, with the headquarters moved to Glasgow and several of Runciman's ships of distinctive if slightly antiquated design being transferred to nominal Anchor Line ownership. In 1968 LINKMOOR became the EUCADIA as seen here, as which she tramped on until 1981. As the Sri Lanka-registered SIGIRYA, she ended her days on Gadani Beach in 1983.

GLENMOOR
Hawthorn, Leslie & Co. Ltd., Newcastle; 1953, 5386gt, 449 feet

The irony of the transfer of Runciman ships was that Anchor Line became owners of vessels much older than the fine cargo liners they had just sold. GLENMOOR, for instance, was 15 years old when repainted in Anchor colours in 1968. She is pictured here off Cardiff in March 1976, a few months before her sale to become the SAUDI FORTUNE under the Singapore flag. Breakers this time were to be in Chittagong, where she arrived in 1982.

HAZELMOOR
Hawthorn, Leslie & Co. Ltd., Newcastle; 1954, 5386gt, 449 feet

Runciman ships acquired Anchor Lines's black funnel - once commonplace but by now something of a rarity. The black hull with the distinctive white line separating the red boot topping soon gave way to a rather ordinary grey hull, although when well-kept as in the case of HAZELMOOR this could look smart. HAZELMOOR reached the grand old age of 24 under Anchor ownership, by when she was fit for little more than scrap, and as FREDDIE 1 she made her way out to Pakistan in 1978.

KIRRIEMOOR
J.L. Thompson and Sons Ltd., Sunderland; 1965, 22198 gt, 646 feet

Anchor Line moved into the age of the bulk carrier with the transfer of KIRRIEMOOR from Runciman ownership in 1968, although the only outward change was the black funnel she eventually acquired. KIRRIEMOOR was sold to London-based Pakistani owners to become AL TAHIR in 1978, being broken up as this in 1985.

BULK CARRIERS

STAR ACADIA
Cammell Laird (Shipbuilding and Engineering) Co. Ltd., Birkenhead; 1970, 19210gt, 564 feet

STAR ACADIA and STAR ASSYRIA were amongst several specialist bulk carriers built by British owners for operation by the Star Shipping Co. Ltd. of Norway. Although the design of the ships with their gantry cranes and huge hatch covers appears to have been successful, Anchor's involvement was less so, and both their ships were sold to Star Shipping in 1975. Since then STAR ACADIA has run under many names: STAR ASAHI, STAR SHAHPOUR, STAR RHODIAN and STAR MALAYSIA. As SAN MATEO VICTORY she sails under the Philippines flag in 1994. *[Fotoflite incorporating Skyfotos]*

CAMERONIA (3)
A/S Burmeister & Wain's Skibsbyggeri, Copenhagen; 1973, 30380gt, 718 feet

In 1973 some revered Anchor names were used for a series of Danish-built bulk carriers. The third, and the largest ship by far, to have born the name CAMERONIA is seen entering the New Waterway in August 1976. Just over a year later she was sold to Norway and very expensively converted to a car carrier, becoming JALANTA and, in 1982, FREEPORT. Under the latter name and the Cypriot flag she is still afloat in 1994.

CALEDONIA (6) *(bottom)*
A/S Burmeister & Wain's Skibsbyggeri, Copenhagen; 1975, 35716gt, 738 feet

Also seen in the New Waterway, CALEDONIA was another short-lived bulker. In 1979 A.P. Moller of Denmark bought her, but some indecision as to the best name has meant her running under a variety of flags as MAERSK NEPTUN, SPRAY TANAO, MAERSK TAURUS and MAERSK BEVERLEE. As plain BEVERLEE she is still in existence under the Bahamas flag.

ELYSIA (5)
Lithgows Ltd., Port Glasgow; 1963, 7689gt, 505 feet

The motor vessel ELYSIA had been built as HIGHLAND for Currie Line Ltd. Their only full-sized cargo liner, she was employed on charter to deep-sea liner companies. She was bought by Anchor Line Ltd. and renamed ELYSIA in 1968 - before their acquisition of Currie - but was sold in 1970. She then sailed under Liberian, Greek and Lebanese flags as ARTEAGA and OLYMPUS until March 1984 when, literally dropping apart, she had to be beached off Japan. She subsequently broke up. *[World Ship Photo Library]*

EGIDIA (2)
Bartram and Sons Ltd., Sunderland; 1961, 7868gt, 461 feet

EGIDIA was the last ship to carry a traditional Anchor Line name. Registered owners were R.I. Shipping Ltd. and R.I. Management Ltd., with Anchor Line Ltd. listed as managers. She had been built as AVISFAITH, and became ALEXANDROS B in 1971. Her brief career as EGIDIA began in 1977, not long before this photograph was taken near the entrance to the Manchester Ship Canal, and ended on her sale to become the Panama-flag SEA VICTORY in 1981. Later names under the same flag were SOUTHDENE and ASTHER, as which she arrived at Spain for breaking up early in 1985.

FINLAND
D.W. Kremer Sohn, Elmshorn, Germany; 1956, 826gt, 225 feet

Currie Line Ltd. of Leith had a long and notable history in the short-sea liner trades, which more or less ended when the company was acquired by Anchor Line in 1969. FINLAND was one of three German-built motor coasters which lasted only until 1971. Sold to Lebanese owners she became successively MARIA PAOLA, KARIM H and SWEET SEA. Under the last of these names she sank after catching fire and being abandoned off Sicily in July 1981.

ZEALAND
Henry Robb Ltd., Leith; 1955, 2167gt, 318 feet

ZEALAND was typical of the engines-amidships short-sea traders which Currie Line favoured. There was no room for her in Anchor's fleet, however, and in 1970 she went out to the Indian Ocean as MALDIVE ENVOY. The shipbreakers of Gadani Beach cut her up in 1981.

GIBSON GAS CARRIERS

QUENTIN
Grangemouth Dockyard Co. Ltd., Grangemouth; 1940, 574gt, 174 feet

Another old-established Leith shipowner, George Gibson & Co. Ltd., was bought by Anchor Line in 1972, but its gas tankers proved more durable than Currie's ships. QUENTIN had been built for Gibsons as a dry-cargo motorship, and was converted to carry liquid ammonia in 1965. Seen here in Gibson's colours at Heysham during July 1971, QUENTIN did not go to the breakers until the ripe old age of 36.

LANRICK
A/B Gavle Varv, Gavle, Sweden; 1957, 1177gt, 252 feet

LANRICK was a further conversion from a Gibson dry cargo vessel, the work being carried out in Holland during 1969. She spent much of her subsequent career on charter to a Spanish gas company, and is seen here at Swansea in May 1981, just one year before she was broken up at Hartlepool.

MELROSE
Heinrich Brand Schiffswerft G.m.b.H. & Co. K.G., Oldenburg, Germany; 1971, 1999gt, 285 feet

MELROSE was one of of a later series of purpose-built gas carriers. In this view on the New Waterway in June 1988, she wears the funnel of Unigas S.A. which is so familiar on gas tankers. She almost survived to be this book's only representative of the current fleet of Anchor Line Ltd., but was sold in 1993, although retaining her Scottish name. [R. Fenton]

SATURNIA

Charles Connell and Co. Ltd., Glasgow; 1910, 8611gt, 456 feet

SATURNIA was one of four ships transferred from Donaldson Line Ltd. to the newly-formed Anchor-Donaldson Ltd. in 1916. This joint venture, in which Anchor Line held a small majority of the shares, operated passenger services from Glasgow to Canadian ports. SATURNIA survived the First World War, and was sold for breaking up at Genoa in 1928.

LETITIA (1)

Scott's Shipbuilding and Engineering Co. Ltd., Greenock; 1912, 8991gt, 470 feet

LETITIA did not serve Anchor-Donaldson Ltd. for long, as she was requisitioned for use as a hospital ship in 1917. On the 1st August 1917 she was carrying a full complement of patients from Liverpool to Canada when she ran into Chebucto Head near Halifax. This could have been a major disaster, but there was only one casualty amongst the 767 on board.

ATHENIA
Fairfield Shipbuilding and Engineering Co. Ltd., Glasgow; 1923, 13465gt, 526 feet

The twin-screw turbine steamer ATHENIA had features in common with contemporary Anchor and Cunard vessels, and it is not surprising that she had been ordered as one of the latter company's "A" class. She is best-known for her tragic end: torpedoed without warning by U 30 within seven hours of the outbreak of the Second World War on 3rd September 1939 whilst on a routine voyage from Liverpool to Montreal. The loss of 112 passengers and crew was a grim foretaste of what unrestricted submarine warfare had in store.

LETITIA (2)
Fairfield Shipbuilding and Engineering Co. Ltd., Glasgow; 1924, 13475gt, 526 feet

ATHENIA's sister LETITIA was destined to have a longer and happier life. Like her sister, she was transferred to the ownership of Donaldson Atlantic Line Ltd. in 1935 when Anchor-Donaldson Ltd. was liquidated. Surviving war service as an armed merchant cruiser, troop transport and hospital ship, she was sold to the Ministry of Transport in 1946. As EMPIRE BRENT and later CAPTAIN COOK she carried troops, war brides and finally emigrants to Australia and New Zealand. She was taken out of service in 1960 and scrapped at Inverkeithing.

EMPIRE CLYDE
William Beardmore & Co. Ltd., Dalmuir, 1920; 16284gt, 575 feet

As related on page 14, the CAMERONIA was refitted after the Second World War and gained a new lease of life as a troop and emigrant carrier. The Ministry of Transport bought her in 1953, renaming her EMPIRE CLYDE but leaving management with Anchor Line. Anchor's colours, seen in the upper photograph, gave way to troopship colours of white hull, blue band and yellow funnel as below. She was broken up at Newport late in 1957.

EMPIRE HALLADALE (below)
A.G. "Vulcan", Hamburg, Germany; 1922, 14056gt, 500 feet

EMPIRE HALLADALE came into British hands as part of the spoils of the Second World War. She had been built for Hamburg-Sudamerikanische D.G. as ANTONIO DELFINO, and had an interesting war: successfully running the British blockade from Brazil in 1940 and helping evacuate East Prussia ahead of the advancing Russians in 1945. The British Ministry of Transport converted her to a troopship and gave her management to Anchor Line. Seen here in May 1951, she trooped for almost ten years, and was broken up at Dalmuir early in 1956.

BROCKLEBANKS - A PROUD HISTORY

Brocklebanks could claim to be the oldest shipowners in the world, and the company took considerable pride in this even after losing its independence. Thos. & Jno. Brocklebank Ltd. was also notable for its long and close association with the trade to Calcutta, for which many of its ships were specially built. All of these were cargo liners: Brocklebanks never entered the passenger business.

The long history began when Daniel Brocklebank left Whitehaven for New England in 1770 to set up in business as a shipbuilder. Although successful in this venture, the hostility between the colonists and King George III persuaded Brocklebank it was prudent to abandon his North American yard and return home to Whitehaven. Here he prospered through his involvement in a number of activities, including shipowning, privateering and shipbuilding.

Legend has it that privateering led to the Brocklebank practice of flying the houseflag from the foremast, the main being required for the letters-of-marque flag. Whatever the truth of this, the half white and half blue flag was certainly a venerable design, and to avoid confusion the international signal flag A had to be designed with a swallowtail: Brocklebanks were not going to change their flag.

On Daniel's death in 1801 the business passed to his sons Thomas and John Brocklebank, and it was the former who opened an office in Liverpool about 1819. Although shipbuilding and other activities continued at Whitehaven for some years, Liverpool was soon to become the centre of operations. Brocklebank ships began to run to India soon after the monopoly of the East India Company began to be eased, but it was only gradually that the company abandoned other trades to concentrate on that for which they became best known, U.K. to Calcutta with calls at other Asian ports.

Brocklebanks were late into steam, almost as if they were waiting for the technology to prove itself. They then embraced it wholeheartedly, sending their staff from Marine Superintendent downwards to sea in other lines' steamers to gain experience before taking delivery of the AMEER in 1889. The last sailing ship, HOLKAR, was sold in 1901.

The circumstances surrounding Brocklebank's loss of independence are complex. By 1911, Harold and Sir Aubrey Brocklebank had come to believe that a family firm could not compete in a world of increasingly large conglomerates. In that year, a chance remark by partners in the merchants and shipowners Edward Bates and Sons led to their being offered Brocklebanks' business. Shares were sold to members of the Bates family, who sat on the board alongside the Brocklebanks. Sir Percy Bates was already a director of the Cunard Steamship Co. Ltd., a connection which probably led to the sale of Anchor Line's Calcutta service to Brocklebanks; Anchor being wholly owned by Cunard. This brought an Anchor Line representative on to the Brocklebank board and, with the retirement of Harold Brocklebank in 1913, Cunard men followed. Formal acquisition of the company by Cunard was now just a matter of course, and in 1919 they bought the shares held by the Brocklebank and Bates families, although two fifths of Brocklebank shares were held by Anchor Line, and were not sold to Cunard until 1940. This takeover had little effect on appearances; indeed, a feature of Brocklebanks' sailing ships reappeared when hulls were repainted from wartime grey to black with a white strake. The major outward sign of the new ownership was the introduction of a service from Calcutta to the U.S.A., with the ships then returning to the U.K. with Cunard cargoes.

Losses during the First World War were more than made up by new-buildings and the acquisition of Well Line and its ships, plus the integration into the fleet of Bates' surviving steamers. Post-war, new ships were ordered for the U.S. service, but the continuing depressed condition of world trade did not justify the expanded fleet. Indeed, the post-war ships were considered too large, and after several years in lay-up four were actually shortened in 1935. Although this surgery was declared a success, any operating savings would have been small, and the main advantage was probably increased handiness when trading up the Hooghly to Calcutta. The

Anchor - Brocklebank Line.

GLASGOW AND LIVERPOOL TO CALCUTTA DIRECT

Taking cargo at through rates from the Bristol Channel.

Steamer.	Closing	Swansea.	Newport.	Glasgow.	Birkenhead.
MATHURA		—	—	—	Apr. 8
STOCKWELL		—	—	Apr. 8	Apr. 15
VERENTIA		—	—	Apr. 22	Apr. 29

For rates and further particulars apply to :—
    ALEXR. HOWDEN & Co., Ltd., 50, Lime Street, London, E.C.3.
    ANCHOR LINE (Henderson Brothers), Ltd., 48, Fenchurch Street, London, E.C.3.
    ANCHOR LINE (Henderson Brothers), Ltd., Manchester and Glasgow.
    MORISON, POLLEXFEN & BLAIR, 8, Victoria Square, Birmingham.
    BAHR, BEHREND & Co., 6, Forster Square, Bradford.
or to the Owners :—**THOS. & JNO. BROCKLEBANK, Ltd.,** Cunard Building, Liverpool.

An Anchor-Brocklebank Line advertisement from 6th April 1926.

inter-war period also saw Brocklebanks experiment with motorships, all of which were failures, and steam turbines continued to drive the fleet for 40 years.

Well-built and fast cargo liners like Brocklebanks' proved invaluable during the Second World War. Losses were again heavy, but the company was allowed to continue building to its own designs and even to develop them, ensuring that the post-war fleet required few wartime standard ships. Despite independence for India and Pakistan, the 1950s were halcyon days for the company, with an energetic building programme producing some handsome ships. Notwithstanding this expansion, vessels had to be chartered in to allow for closure of Suez, extra ports of call and operation of certain Harrison Line services which Brocklebanks acquired.

The formation of Cunard-Brocklebank Ltd. in 1968 marked a watershed in the company's affairs. By now it was becoming apparent that trends such as containerisation and increasing nationalism in shipping were altering traditional trading patterns. The last ship built for Brocklebanks emerged in that year, although transfers of Cunard and Port Line ships kept numbers up for a time. The name Thos. & Jno. Brocklebank Ltd. was gradually dropped, as ships were registered under Cunard Steamship Co. Ltd. or Cunard-Brocklebank Ltd.

Brocklebank's black funnel with blue-over-white bands was more widely used, however, and was applied to a group of bulk carriers. The last cargo liner both to wear Brocklebank colours and carry a name beginning MA - the test for inclusion in this book - was sold in 1983. It was 213 years since Daniel Brocklebank had entered the shipping business.

SOURCES

Many books have been consulted whilst compiling the histories and captions, notably R.S. McLellan's *Anchor Line 1856-1956* and J.F. Gibson's two-volume *Brocklebanks 1770-1950. From Cumberland to Cape Horn* by D. Hollett revisits the Brocklebank story using contemporary sources, but finishes with the end of sail. Fleet lists have given useful guidance, especially that in Duncan Haws' *Merchant Fleets 9: Anchor Line* (a book which also provides a history of Anchor's later years) and D.E. Stillwell's excellent work on Brocklebanks in *Sea Breezes* for February and March 1984. All the ships' data and histories have been checked in reference books, particularly *Lloyds Registers* and - for post-Second World War scrappings - *Marine News*. Use of the resources of the World Ship Society's Central Record and Lloyds Register of Shipping is gratefully acknowledged.

EARLY STEAMERS

IRAK
Workman, Clark and Co. Ltd., Belfast; 1902, 8121gt, 501 feet

The sale of Brocklebank shares to partners in Edward Bates and Co. in 1911 resulted in Bates' IRAK - seen here - being chartered to Brocklebank and renamed MANDASOR (1). She was sold to Hamburg Amerika in 1912 to become BELGIA, but was captured by Britain, reputedly as the first prize of the war. Germany had its revenge, however, and as HUNTSTRICK she was torpedoed by U 39 off Cape Spartel, Morocco in June 1917.

AMEER
Harland and Wolff Ltd., Belfast; 1889, 4014gt, 400 feet

Brocklebank's first venture into steam, AMEER had an up-to-date triple-expansion engine but still carried a full set of sails. When the company bought shares in Shire Line in 1906, several ships were renamed to operate their services, and AMEER became CARDIGANSHIRE. In 1911 she was sold to Japan as HAKUSHIKA MARU and later IDE MARU. Under Hong Kong ownership she reverted to CARDIGANSHIRE in 1919, and then spent a few years owned in Manila as PACO FIGUERIAS until broken up in 1923.

MAHRONDA (1) (above)
and FRATERNITAS (bottom)
Harland and Wolff Ltd., Belfast; 1905, 7630gt, 470 feet

Brocklebanks moved cautiously away from sail, and their first large steamer order was for four with quadruple-expansion engines, beginning with the first MAHRONDA. She was the only one of the quartet to remain in Brocklebank ownership after the First World War, and her subsequent career was unusual. After sale to Norwegian owners in 1923 she was converted into a whale factory ship and renamed SIR JAMES CLARK ROSS. In 1930 she became FRATERNITAS under

the management of A.P. Moller of Copenhagen, although the accompanying photograph shows her in the funnel colours of a Norwegian company. Her last name was UNIWALECO, adopted when sold to South African owners in 1937. Wartime saw her used as a tanker, and she was carrying a cargo of fuel oil from Curacoa to Freetown when torpedoed by U 161 off the West Indies on 7th March 1942. *[lower: A. Duncan]*

37

ANCHORIA
Alexander Stephen and Sons Ltd., Linthouse; 1911, 5430gt, 410 feet

Following Anchor Line's acquisition by Cunard, their Calcuttta conference rights were sold to Brocklebanks, together with four ships. Two of these - ANCHORIA and MEDIA - were almost new: the former being seen here in the Mersey on 15th September 1934. Although still looking well, just a year later she was sold to Cardiff owners and traded in under the "Scrap and Build" scheme, being demolished at Osaka in March 1936.

MEDIA
Alexander Stephen and Sons Ltd., Linthouse; 1911; 5437gt, 410 feet

The Anchor Line ships retained their names, but were registered in Brocklebank ownership and painted in their colours. In 1935 MEDIA was sold to Italy and became VELOCE. She was to become a war loss, bombed and sunk off Tunisia on 2nd December 1942 whilst attempting to supply fuel to Tripoli.

MALAKUTA
Charles Connell and Co. Ltd., Scotstoun; 1914, 7205gt, 470 feet

The last pre-war deliveries to Brocklebanks were a pair of outwardly similar ships. MALAKUTA was given conventional steam reciprocating machinery, and had the shorter Brocklebank career. Sold in 1935 she became the Chinese SHENG HO, being taken by Japan as SEIWA MARU three years later. As this she was a victim of Japan's almost complete lack of convoy protection, when sunk by U.S. carrier aircraft off the Philippines on 13th November 1944. *[WSS Brownell Collection]*

MAHANADA (2)
Charles Connell and Co. Ltd., Scotstoun; 1914, 7196gt, 470 feet

MAHANADA was Brocklebank's first use of turbine machinery, and, judging by her longer Brocklebank career than the reciprocating-engined MALAKUTA, this must have been considered a success. MAHANADA was lost on 26th February 1942, when bombed and set on fire by a Heinkel He-111 whilst in a convoy west of Ireland. She was on a voyage from Manchester to Port Said with a cargo consisting mainly of railway locomotives.

HOLYWELL

Hawthorn, Leslie & Co. Ltd., Newcastle; 1907, 4867gt, 401 feet

The Well Line was bought in 1916; its service from the east coast of the U.K. and the Continent complementing that of Brocklebanks from the west coast. Although absorbed into the Brocklebank fleet the six Well Line ships retained their names, in the case of HOLYWELL until she was broken up at Bo'ness in 1933.

STOCKWELL

Sir J. Laing and Sons Ltd., Sunderland; 1914, 5643gt, 425 feet

Well Line's STOCKWELL certainly looked well in Brocklebank's colours, particularly with the broad white band around the hull; a sailing ship practice adopted when the steamers were repainted after the First World War. When sold in 1938, STOCKWELL's name was changed almost at a stroke, becoming Billmeir's STANWELL. Her end was somewhat ignominious: sunk as part of the Gooseberry Harbour at Arromanches in June 1944.

MAHRATTA (2)
R. Duncan and Co. Ltd., Port Glasgow; 1917, 6690gt, 445 feet

Replacements for Brocklebank's First World War losses came from a variety of yards, but all showed an attention to design and indeed elegance that belied the country's desperate need for ships. MAHRATTA just survived into the next war: arriving home from Calcutta she ran on to the Goodwin Sands on 6th October 1939 whilst awaiting a pilot and broke her back. Curiously, the previous ship of this name had also been lost on the Goodwins, 30 years before.

MAKALLA (1)
R. Duncan and Co. Ltd., Port Glasgow; 1918, 6781gt, 445 feet

MAKALLA was not an exact copy of MAHRATTA: many detail differences are apparent, particularly the ventilators immediately ahead of the bridge. For many years MAKALLA was Brocklebank's apprentice training ship, although no extra accommodation is apparent. On 23rd August 1940 she became the company's first loss through bombing, sunk in a determined attack on her convoy by the Luftwaffe. She was off the north of Scotland, bound from London to Calcutta via Durban.

MAIHAR (1)
Russell and Co., Port Glasgow; 1917, 8071gt, 470 feet

Although war-built and with triple-expansion engines, MAIHAR was to have a remarkable career in Brocklebank ownership, surviving into the decade which saw the container ship arrive. The small hatches by the funnel were for coal bunkers, but when MAIHAR was converted to an oil-burner the space was turned into accommodation for Lascar crews being brought from Calcutta to Glasgow to join new ships. MAIHAR was not sold until 1962, when as the Lebanese-flag CAPELLA she made a last east bound voyage, arriving at a Japanese breaker's yard in May 1962.

MAHSUD (1)
Russell and Co., Port Glasgow; 1917, 8077gt, 470 feet

The MAHSUD was another Brocklebank ship with an apparently charmed life. She survived an Atlantic voyage with no rudder in 1918, and an attack by Italian divers with limpet mines at Gibraltar in 1943. After the latter adventure she required a new bottom, engines and boilers, which kept her in service until May 1955. She was then sold to C.Y. Tung, becoming the Panama CASSIAN MARINER and PACIFIC MARINER in quick succession, before being broken up in Japan in 1959.

MACHARDA (1)
Russell and Co., Port Glasgow; 1918, 10464gt, 518 feet

Although a size larger than MAIHAR, one has to search hard for detail differences in the MACHARDA's appearance. A major difference was below decks, where MACHARDA had a quadruple-expansion engine which was originally destined for an Austrian Lloyd vessel. In contrast to MAIHAR, she was to have a notably brief career and was sold to Japanese breakers in 1932 after serving for a mere 14 years: her large size counting against her during the lean years between the wars.

MAIMYO
Russell and Co., Port Glasgow; 1917, 6289gt, 423 feet

The MAIMYO has little in common with the other Russell-built ships on this page. Her small size would have made her useful to the company in the 1930s, but she became a peacetime casualty, off Ceylon on 24th December 1936 whilst homeward bound from Calcutta.

MANAAR (1)
Charles Connell and Co. Ltd., Scotstoun; 1917, 7242gt, 470 feet

The turbine steamer MANAAR was Brocklebank's first loss due to enemy action during the Second World War. The conflict was only days old when, bound from Liverpool to Calcutta, she encountered U 38 off Portugal on 6th September 1939. The MANAAR came off worst in the ensuing gun fight, which ended with her being abandoned and torpedoed.

MASIRAH (1)
Charles Connell and Co. Ltd., Port Glasgow; 1919, 6836gt, 448 feet

MASIRAH seems to have had a peaceful career. Her triple-expansion engines drove her sedately along until she arrived for scrap at Troon on 25th February 1954, a coal-burner to the end.

MALAKAND (2)
Lithgows Ltd., Port Glasgow; 1919, 7649gt, 470 feet

The serenity of the sky over the Mersey in this photograph provides a counterpoint to the violence of MALAKAND's end. During the night of the 3rd/4th May 1941, when Liverpool suffered its worst air raid, she was lying in No. 2 Branch of Huskisson Dock having loaded ammunition. Incendiary and high explosive bombs set the adjacent shed on fire and, despite all the crew could do, the fire quickly spread to the MALAKAND. It seems to have been impossible to scuttle the ship, and about an hour after sunrise she blew up. The devastation was such that Huskisson No. 2 Branch was filled in shortly afterwards, forming a grave for the remains of MALAKAND.

MATHERAN (2)
Lithgows Ltd., Port Glasgow; 1919, 7653gt, 470 feet

Like her sister MALAKAND, MATHERAN was a war loss, torpedoed by U 38 - which had also despatched MANAAR - on 19th October 1940 whilst in a convoy from Halifax to the U.K. The survivors' ordeal continued as their rescue ship LOCH LOMOND was herself torpedoed the next day, although fortunately without loss of life.

MAGDAPUR (1)

Lithgows Ltd., Port Glasgow; 1921, 9237gt, 499 feet

The MAGDAPUR is shown here as built. She and three other Brocklebank ships were considered uneconomically large for the depressed trading conditions of the 1930s, and were sent to Smith's Dock in 1935 to be shortened. In the case of MAGDAPUR a 26-foot section aft of the bridge and ahead of the kingposts was removed. She was an early victim of a mine: sunk off Aldeburgh on 10th September 1939 when coasting from South Shields to Southampton. In the photograph she must be on an Anchor Brocklebank Line sailing: note the Anchor Line houseflag at the main whilst the Brocklebank flag is at its traditional position on the foremast.

MANIPUR (2)

Lithgows Ltd., Port Glasgow; 1920, 6652gt, 473 feet

In contrast, the MAGDAPUR's sister MANIPUR appears here as shortened in 1935: the photo on the title page shows her as built. She too was a war loss, torpedoed and sunk by U 57 off Cape Wrath on 17th July 1940 whilst in a homeward-bound Halifax convoy.

MANGALORE

Charles Connell and Co. Ltd., Scotstoun; 1920, 9751gt/8836 gt, 518 feet/480 feet

In the case of the MANGALORE, shortening by 38 feet also involved removing a pair of kingposts, as these before-and-after views reveal. Although the slab sides matched, there was a step on the hulls of the shortened ships where the two parts had been joined. MANGALORE was another mine victim, blown up off Spurn Point on the 24th November 1939, fortunately without loss of life. *[lower: WSS Brownell Collection]*

D.W. WILLIAMS
W.J. Yarwood and Sons Ltd., Northwich; 1920, 177gt, 96 feet

D.W. WILLIAMS was one of two steam derrick barges used to attend the company's ships on Merseyside, and named after senior managers. Her unglamorous life continued following her sale to the Mersey Docks and Harbour Board in 1950, as seen here in April 1960. Hardly modern when built, she was nevertheless still afloat in the 1970s.

FULLAGAR
Cammell, Laird and Co. Ltd., Birkenhead; 1920, 398gt, 150 feet

The coaster FULLAGAR was a doubly-innovative ship. She was a pioneer of all-welded construction and was propelled - although rather briefly - by a novel oil engine whose inventor's name she carried. This engine proved a failure, and after a little over a year she was sold and given a more conventional Beardmore diesel. This stood her in good stead throughout a subsequent, adventurous career. After running on the U.K. coast as CARIA, in 1925 she went to British Columbia to work for a cement company as SHEAN. Venturing south to Mexico in 1935 she became CEDROS, but was run down and sunk south off Ensenada in August 1937. The photograph was taken on 29th June 1920 during trials in the Mersey. *[Williamson Art Gallery and Museum]*

DAGA ex-MALIA

William Hamilton and Co. Ltd., Port Glasgow; 1921, 3872gt, 350 feet

Having installed an oil engine in the FULLAGAR, Brocklebank repeated the experiment in the full-sized MALIA. This was no more successful, and her two Cammell Laird-Fullagar engines were replaced in 1923. Soon after her sale to become the DAGA of Henderson Line in 1927 she was again re-engined. Sold to Bank Line as KELVINBANK in 1934, she was torpedoed by U 510 off South America on 9th March 1943.

LYCIA

Dunlop, Bremner and Co. Ltd., Port Glasgow; 1924, 2338gt, 300 feet

LYCIA was a further experiment with motor power, but was quickly returned to her builders as underpowered, making this photograph of her in Brocklebank colours of considerable historic interest. In 1926 she was sold to the Cape York Motorship Co. Ltd., which was later to be managed by the Lyle Shipping Co. Ltd. She was sunk as a blockship at Scapa Flow early in 1941 - a fate to which her unreliable engines condemned her.

MAHRONDA (2)
William Hamilton and Co. Ltd., Port Glasgow; 1925, 7880gt, 470 feet
Despite a contracting pattern of world trade, Brocklebanks expanded their services in the 1920s with monthly sailings from Calcutta to the U.S.A. and on to the U.K. MAHRONDA and MAHOUT were two of the five extra ships ordered for the service. MAHRONDA was torpedoed by the Japanese submarine I 20 off Mozambique on 11th June 1942 when bound from Liverpool to Karachi.

MAHOUT (1)
William Hamilton and Co. Ltd., Port Glasgow; 1925, 7880gt, 470 feet

MAHOUT survived to be scrapped at Blyth where she arrived in March 1961, a coal-burner to the end. The upper photograph shows her in Australian waters, on charter to Port Line. Her post-war appearance was somewhat marred by her lack of a main topmast and this meant her mast head light was actually fixed to the funnel, although this is obscured by coal smoke in the lower view.

MARKHOR (1)
William Hamilton and Co. Ltd., Port Glasgow; 1929, 7835gt, 470 feet

The 1920s saw Brocklebanks begin a long and fruitful relationship with the Clydeside yard of William Hamilton and Co. Ltd. MARKHOR was a turbine-driven steamer capable of over 13 knots loaded. She served Brocklebanks well, and went to Hong Kong owners as MANFHOR in 1960, being broken up during the next year. She is seen here in June 1956.

MARWARRI (2)
William Hamilton and Co. Ltd., Port Glasgow; 1935, 8063gt, 471 feet

MARWARRI was a refinement of MARKHOR, with a little extra speed. She was notable for having the first refrigerated cargo space on a Brocklebank ship, and for her propensity to roll. She proved a good investment, although she had to be re-engined after being mined in 1939. MARWARRI arrived at Hong Kong to be scrapped in May 1963, the photograph being taken ten years earlier.

MALANCHA (2)
William Hamilton and Co. Ltd., Port Glasgow; 1937, 8124gt, 496 feet

Having produced a sound design, Brocklebanks and Hamiltons perpetuated it, and MALANCHA differed from MARWARRI only in having a more raked stem. In terms of equipment she was something of an anachronism, however, with wooden hatch covers, steam winches and cold running water only in senior officers' cabins. MALANCHA is seen here at New Orleans on 30th March 1957. In 1962 she was sold and, with her name shortened to MALAN, made a final voyage to the breakers, arriving at Hong Kong in March.

MACHARDA (2)
William Hamilton and Co. Ltd., Port Glasgow; 1938, 7998gt, 496 feet

MACHARDA's career ran in parallel with her sister MALANCHA's, and she too was broken up at Hong Kong in 1962.

MATHERAN (3)

William Hamilton and Co. Ltd., Port Glasgow; 1942, 8007gt, 494 feet

Brocklebanks were allowed to continue ordering ships to their own design during the Second World War, and there were several copies of pre-war ships, differing largely in having smaller funnels. MATHERAN traded until sold to Japanese breakers in 1963, arriving at Osaka during May.

MALAKAND (3)

William Hamilton and Co. Ltd., Port Glasgow; 1942, 8030gt, 494 feet

The name of the war-loss MALAKAND was quickly perpetuated. The later ship came to a more peaceful end, however, arriving at Kaohsiung to be scrapped on 13th December 1966.

MAHANADA (3)
William Hamilton and Co. Ltd., Port Glasgow; 1943, 8971gt, 505 feet

In general, owners were only permitted to build to their own order during the Second World War if they did so to an existing design. However, Brocklebank's later war construction was to a new layout, with accommodation alongside the centre hold. This development was allowed because the greatly increased accommodation - although spartan - was useful in wartime. No. 3 hatch could be trunked up to the boat deck, now that the company's full acceptance of oil-firing meant that no provision was needed for coal bunkers. The first ship completed to this design, MAHANADA originally had a good complement of anti-aircraft weapons. She is seen here in August 1954: she lasted until 1967 when she became CORONA for a few months prior to being demolished in Taiwan.

MAGDAPUR (2)
William Hamilton and Co. Ltd., Port Glasgow; 1945, 9142gt, 504 feet

MAGDAPUR saw a further refinement of the Hamilton ships. Externally, she had two sets of kingposts to serve the centre hold, and steel hatch covers. Internally, high pressure boilers allowed smaller turbines to be fitted, reducing the size of the engine room - and thus the target it offered to submarines. This fine photo, taken during the summer of 1954, shows the two bore pipes in her stern. These were used to split the anchor cable when the ships were moored in the Hooghly, a measure necessary to withstand the river's powerful tidal bore. In 1970 MAGDAPUR followed her predecessors, her name being truncated to MAGDA for her voyage to the breakers.

MANIPUR (3)
William Hamilton and Co. Ltd., Port Glasgow; 1945, 9233 gt, 504 feet

MANIPUR is seen here on her native Clyde: another product of the remarkably durable relationship between Brocklebanks and the Port Glasgow builders. Features which the crews of these ships appreciated were hot and cold running water in all cabins, and electric winches which made cargo working much quieter. MANIPUR was broken up at Whampoa, arriving there on 6th January 1967.

MAIDAN (3)
William Hamilton and Co. Ltd., Port Glasgow; 1946, 8533 gt, 504 feet

Careful comparison of the two photographs on this page will reveal a subtle distinction between the ships. MAIDAN was the first Brocklebank ship to dispense with cowl ventilators for the holds, having mechanical ventilation throughout. In 1969 she was sold to Troodos Shipping and Trading Ltd. to become the Cyprus-flag PRETTY. She was renamed TAIGHETOS in 1972, but soon after suffered grounding damage off Djibouti and was broken up in Taiwan. This photograph was taken in Dutch waters in June 1968.

MAHRONDA (3)
William Hamilton and Co. Ltd., Port Glasgow; 1947, 8495gt, 504 feet

With barely any way on, MAHRONDA awaits a pilot. At the end of her Brocklebank career in 1969 she was sold and registered in Cyprus as LUCKY. It proved an inappropriate name: on 14th May 1970 she was severely damaged by fire at Rotterdam, and was fit only for demolition. She arrived under tow at Split, Yugoslavia in December 1970.

MANAAR (3)
William Hamilton and Co. Ltd., Port Glasgow; 1950, 8996gt, 508 feet

Brocklebank's adherence to turbine-driven cargo liners had the effect of making them rather difficult to sell when they reached the end of their careers, buyers preferring more economical motor ships. Like others of her class, MANAAR was sold directly out of the fleet to the scrappers, arriving at Taiwan in July 1971. The photograph dates from 1960.

MAHSEER (2)
William Hamilton and Co. Ltd., Port Glasgow; 1948, 8945gt, 508 feet

In some of the last of the long sequence of split-superstructure ships from Port Glasgow, the main mast was replaced by a pair of kingposts, as seen in the two ships on this page. This class were fitted with dryers in the larger holds to prevent sweat damage to the cargo, an important consideration when loading during a south west monsoon. MAHSEER's career was uncomplicated: after 25 years' service she was sold to Pakistani breakers, arriving at Karachi in June 1975.

MATRA (3)
William Hamilton and Co. Ltd., Port Glasgow; 1949, 8954gt, 508 feet

The Brocklebank turbine ships which did find other buyers tended to have short careers. MATRA became AEGIS SAVE 1 in 1971 on her sale to the Papalios organisation, but in February 1972 arrived at Gandia in Spain to be broken up.

MANDASOR (3)
William Gray and Co. Ltd., West Hartlepool; 1944, 7071gt, 446 feet

With a steady flow of ships to their own design from 1942 onwards, Brocklebanks needed to buy few wartime standard ships. The steamer EMPIRE MALACCA - almost a Brocklebank name itself - was managed for the Ministry of War Transport from new until 1946, when she was bought and renamed MANDASOR. Being rather slow, she was an early disposal, and was sold to the Tsavliris group in 1962 to run as FOTINI TSAVLIRIS and as FREE TRADER. Following a grounding off the Dutch coast in September 1970 she was laid up in Piraeus until broken up in Turkey during 1972.

MALABAR (2)
J.A. Jones Construction Co. Inc., Brunswick, Georgia, U.S.A.; 1943, 7280gt, 441 feet

MALABAR was Brocklebank's only Liberty. Launched as PATRICK D. MORRISSEY, she had been managed for the Ministry as SAMDEE until her purchase in 1947. Like other Liberties, she was appreciated by her crews for having more advanced features than contemporary British ships. MALABAR was sold to Greek owners in 1961, and steamed on as the OMONIA until broken up in Japan during 1967.

MAKALLA (2)

Canadian Vickers Ltd., Montreal, Canada; 1941, 7122gt, 424 feet

FORT VILLE MARIE was the first Fort-type delivered, and was one of four managed by Brocklebanks, whose staff nicknamed her "Vile Mary". She was purchased and renamed MAKALLA in 1946, as seen in this smoky shot from July 1949. Unusually for a Fort, she went straight from liner company to breakers, being demolished at Ghent during 1963.

MAHSUD (2)

West Coast Shipbuilders Ltd., Vancouver, Canada; 1943, 7164gt, 439 feet

The company's second Fort was something of a distress purchase, acquired in 1956 when voyages suddenly lengthened after the closure of the Suez Canal. She had already carried the names FORT ENTERPRISE, TAVISTOCK and SOUTHWICK, all under the British flag. As MAHSUD she lasted only until 1961, being sold to the World Wide Shipping Group of Hong Kong and carrying the names MARINE TRAVELLER, BANDAHARA and OTONE. She was demolished in Japan during 1966.

CHARTERS

MANDAGALA

Bethlehem-Fairfield Shipyard Inc., Baltimore, U.S.A.; 1945, 7681gt, 455 feet

In 1957 the Victory-type BRITISH PRINCE, ex-STAMFORD VICTORY, was time-chartered from Furness, Withy & Co. Ltd. and given full Brocklebank colours as MANDAGALA. With the charter over in 1960, she did not revert to her old name but was sold to become ORIENT TRADER under the Greek flag. As this she was damaged by fire at Toronto in July 1965, and almost a year later scrapped in Spain. *[Fotoflite incorporating Skyfotos]*

MADULSIMA

Harland and Wolff Ltd., Glasgow; 1956, 8495gt, 466 feet

In contrast to MANDAGALA, ROWANMORE of Johnson Warren Lines Ltd. had only her funnel repainted when she was chartered in 1958, although she adopted the Brocklebank-style name MADULSIMA. She reverted to ROWANMORE in 1961, and later ran as ANDRIANA I and MARJORIE Y before arriving in Spain to be broken up at the end of 1979. *[A. Duncan]*

MALABAR (3)

Cammell, Laird and Co. (Shipbuilders & Engineering) Ltd., Birkenhead; 1954, 1202gt, 256 feet

During the 1960s, Brocklebanks took over responsibility for Cunard services to the Mediterranean, for which they chartered several small motor vessels. CHESHIRE COAST was owned by the Belfast Steamship Co. Ltd. and was renamed MALABAR for a short period in 1967. She was to have further Mediterranean adventures, running for Prince Line Ltd. as SPARTAN PRINCE. Her last years were spent as the Cyprus-owned VENTURE and AZELIA before going for scrap at Cartagena in 1980.

MAKALLA (3) (top)
Hall, Russell and Co. Ltd., Aberdeen; 1948, 1265gt, 227 feet

During 1967 and 1968 a Brocklebank charter gave Coast Lines' CALEDONIAN COAST and her crew a taste of the Mediterranean climate. Despite the relatively short time on hire, she received a full Brocklebank repaint and the name MAKALLA. Sold on coming off hire, she became the Kuwait-owned AHMADI COAST, as which she was broken up in Spain during 1974.

MAKALLA (4)
Norderwerft Koser and Meyer, Hamburg, Germany; 1955, 1801gt, 291 feet

Slightly larger ships were chartered for the Mediterranean trade from 1969 to 1972. The MAKALLA, seen here in the Bristol Channel in May 1970, had been the German JOHN SCHRODER, but was sold to Greece in 1969. Unusually, she continued trading as MAKALLA after the charter had ended. Renamed AMALIA in 1977, she became a total loss that year whilst under repair at Perama.

COMPOSITE SUPERSTRUCTURE

MAIPURA
William Hamilton and Co. Ltd., Port Glasgow; 1952, 9748gt, 508 feet

MAIPURA was Brocklebank's first post-war building with a composite superstructure like that of a Liberty: a design adopted to give a longer foredeck for carrying the bulkier items of deck cargo which were increasingly being shipped. Her funnel was a notable structure: soon after completion it was heightened by some 12 feet to try to prevent fumes entering the after accommodation. MAIPURA was destined to remain a one-off, but the design was further developed into the MASKELIYA class. MAIPURA herself went under the Panama flag in 1972 as LIBERTY RETAILER, and was broken up in Taiwan during 1974.

MASKELIYA
William Hamilton and Co. Ltd., Port Glasgow; 1954, 7350gt, 472 feet

In terms of elegance, British cargo liner design reached its zenith in the 1950s, and the MASKELIYA class could hold their own in any company. They were built mainly for the developing trade from India to the southern U.S.A. MASKELIYA had a relatively short career, however, and became the Panama-flag OCEAN JOY in 1969, being broken up in Taiwan just three years later.

MAKRANA
William Hamilton and Co. Ltd., Port Glasgow; 1957, 8745gt, 497 feet

This view of MAKRANA passing Dover shows the pronounced funnel dome which was inspired by a similar feature on contemporary Cunard liners. However, those who served on the ships suggest it failed to prevent soot falling on deck. MAKRANA was sold to the Papalios group in 1971, running under the Cypriot flag as AEGIS GLORY and later AEGIS ETERNITY. It was not, however, an eternity before she was broken up: Chinese mainland breakers claimed her in April 1974. *[Fotoflite incorporating Skyfotos]*

MASIRAH (2)
William Hamilton and Co. Ltd., Port Glasgow; 1957, 8733gt, 497 feet

This class introduced bipod masts to the Brocklebank fleet, a concept which eliminated the need for mast stays, although Suez Canal pilots complained that the bipods obstructed the view forward. Here MASIRAH waits in the Albert Dock, Birkenhead, having just locked in from the Mersey. She had 1,000 horsepower less than other members of the class, reducing her speed by one knot to 15. MASIRAH was sold to the Marchessini group in 1972 and became EURYSTHENES. She grounded off the Philippines in April 1974, but although refloated was beyond economical repair and went to Taiwanese breakers in November 1974.

MAWANA
William Hamilton and Co. Ltd., Port Glasgow; 1958, 8744gt, 497 feet

MAWANA is seen in Dutch waters in June 1966; the Dutch courtesy ensign displacing the Brocklebank houseflag from the fore topmast. The life of members of this class after their sale by Brocklebanks tended to be short, the 50 tons of fuel consumed by their turbines each day making them unattractive to further owners. In 1971 MAWANA joined other members of her class in the Papalios group as the Greek-registered AEGIS LEGEND, but was broken up in Japan during 1974. She was only 16.

MANGLA
William Hamilton and Co. Ltd., Port Glasgow; 1959, 8805gt, 497 feet

In the Thames MANGLA has no courtesy ensign to fly, and her houseflag can take a prominent position. Sold to Marchessini as EURYPYLUS in 1972, she had a serious explosion in her engine room in the Pacific during November 1975. She was fit only for scrap, arriving at Kaohsiung under tow in April 1976.

MATHURA (2) *(top)* **and EURYTION** *(bottom)*
William Hamilton and Co. Ltd., Port Glasgow; 1960, 8782 gt, 497 feet

The Cunard-type funnel of MATHURA is seen here in Cunard colours, in which she looks very well. It is interesting to note how her appearance was altered by repainting in the colours of Marchessini Lines, who bought her in 1972. In 1976 Marchessini sold the ship to Kuwait owners who renamed her ALWAHA. At Aden in September 1977 she became another victim of an engine room fire, suggesting that ageing boilers could be a liability. Laid up for over a year, she was then towed to Gadani Beach for scrap. The photograph of EURYTION was taken in the New Waterway in July 1974.

MAHOUT (2)
Alexander Stephens and Sons Ltd., Glasgow; 1963, 6867gt, 480 feet

With the end of the long-standing relationship with William Hamilton, design changed - and hardly for the better in aesthetic terms. In this July 1974 view in the New Waterway, MAHOUT does not even have a fore topmast from which to fly her houseflag. An innovation for the company was bridge control of the main engine, although this was viewed with suspicion by her crews. The builders marketed the system under the name Mahout Engine Control. MAHOUT was sold in 1978, becoming first AGLAOS and later EVAGELIA S, both Greek-owned and registered. Sadly, EVAGELIA S became a war loss: bombed by Iraqi aircraft near Bandar Khomeini in September 1982.

MARKHOR (2)
Alexander Stephens and Sons Ltd., Glasgow; 1963, 6867gt, 480 feet

The first diesel-driven Brocklebank ships for four decades, MAHOUT and MARKHOR had longer lives in the fleet than their turbine-driven predecessors. MARKHOR was sold in 1976 but chartered back until 1981. In 1982 she became the Panama-flag KARA UNICORN, but was broken up at Dalian in China during 1984.

MAHSUD (3)
A/B Lindholmens Varv., Gothenburg, Sweden; 1968, 9416gt, 505 feet

Traditional builders, along with traditional cargo gear, were abandoned with the MAHSUD and MAIHAR of 1968. Times they were achanging fast, and after only ten years these 17-knot sisters were laid up on the Fal, overtaken by container ships. Later in 1978 MAHSUD was sold to become the TURQUOISE. She was placed under the Panama flag, and registered under the ownership of a Hong Kong company, which was ostensibly controlled from Japan. In 1981, and without change of name or flag, it became apparent that she was owned by the Socialist Republic of Vietnam, to whose registry she was transferred in 1986 to become NINH GIANG. She arrived at Alang for scrap early in 1990.

MAIHAR (2)
A/B Lindholmens Varv., Gothenburg, Sweden; 1968, 9416gt, 505 feet
The white hull with a blue band was another innovation introduced in 1968, and some older members of the fleet were repainted to match. Seen here on charter, MAIHAR's career initially parallelled that of her sister, being sold and rechristened GARNET in 1978. In December 1981, however, she collided with a tanker off Port Said and had to be beached, becoming a constructive total loss.

MACHARDA (3)
William Hamilton and Co. Ltd., Port Glasgow; 1960, 7004gt, 490 feet

Some elegance returned to the Brocklebank fleet in 1969 with the transfer of several ships from the Cunard Steamship Co. Ltd. MACHARDA had been ANDANIA, made redundant by the arrival of specialised container ships on the North Atlantic. Service on Brocklebank's Indian routes was brief, however, and in 1971 MACHARDA went under the Panama flag as the Hong Kong-owned HUMI MAHIS. Subsequent names under mainland Chinese ownership were YUNGJIHAN and HONG QI 107. She was broken up in China during 1986.

[V.H. Young & L.A. Sawyer]

MALANCHA (3)
William Hamilton and Co. Ltd., Port Glasgow; 1960, 6658gt, 490 feet

MACHARDA and MALANCHA came from the same builder as the MASKELIYA class, hence the general similarity in layout. Built as Cunard's ALAUNIA, MALANCHA's career parallelled that of MACHARDA, being sold to the same owners in the same years and taking the names HUMI NASITA, YUNGMING and HONG QI 108, and being deleted from Lloyds Register in 1993. MALANCHA was photographed in May 1971.

MANIPUR (4)
Caledon Shipbuilding and Engineering Co. Ltd., Dundee; 1964, 8783gt, 517 feet

Further Cunard cast-offs came in 1970; IVERNIA becoming MANIPUR and being lengthened by Swan, Hunter. She is seen here in June 1973, but unfortunately without Brocklebank's white hull ribbon. In 1971 she was briefly renamed CONCORDIA MANIPUR whilst on charter to Christian Haaland of Norway. Following disposal in 1977 she became PHILIPPA in the fleet of the Swiss-based Mediterranean Shipping Co. S.A. She arrived at Chittagong for demolition in February 1985.

MAHRONDA (4)
J. Readhead and Sons, South Shields; 1964, 8783gt, 517 feet

Seen in May 1976, MAHRONDA was previously Cunard's SAXONIA. Like her sister she was chartered to Christian Haaland for a few months in 1982, becoming CONCORDIA FOSS. After a short lay-up in the Fal she became the Singapore-owned NEW DEER in 1977 and was broken up in China in 1983.

MATANGI
Harland and Wolff Ltd., Belfast; 1961, 10486gt, 500 feet

In their final years Brocklebanks became the last British operators of several Port Line ships. Built as PORT ST. LAWRENCE, MATANGI is seen on the Tees in December 1975, soon after receiving a name which sounds more Maori than Indian. After seven years in Brocklebank service she was sold to Malta as NORDAVE, but in April 1983 arrived at the ships' graveyard at Gadani Beach.

MASIR ex-MASIRAH (2)
Harland and Wolff Ltd., Belfast; 1961, 10487gt, 500 feet

PORT ALFRED was transferred to Brocklebank's Indian services in 1975, but not renamed MASIRAH until 1978. In 1982 she was sold to Greek owners, who registered her in Gibraltar as MASIR. In this view she is laid up at Piraeus in October 1984. Leaving lay-up in March 1986, she made one trip to northern Europe before being sold to Indian shipbreakers.

MANAAR (4)
Alexander Stephens and Sons, Glasgow; 1968, 16275gt, 612 feet

PORT CHALMERS was transferred to Brocklebanks in 1981 as a way of reducing crew costs: by agreement with British unions the company could employ Indian seamen. She remained on Port Line services, however, and is seen here at Bluff, New Zealand in March 1982. During the next year she became the Greek-owned GOLDEN GLORY, lasting until 1985 when broken up at Shanghai.

MATRA (4) *(middle)*
Upper Clyde Shipbuilders Ltd., Linthouse; 1968, 16275gt, 612 feet

MATRA ex-PORT CAROLINE is seen in the Foveaux Strait on a stormy day in January 1982. She was one of the last two cargo liners in Brocklebank colours when sold in 1983, after which she ran as GOLDEN DOLPHIN until demolished at Shanghai in 1985. *[V.H. Young & L.A. Sawyer]*

INDEX OF SHIPS
The names of ships which appear in photographs are shown in capitals.

MATHURA (1)
Charles Connell and Co. Ltd., Scotstoun; 1920, 8890gt, 480 feet

This photograph of MATHURA is dated 14th August 1938, after her shortening. Of the quartet which received this treatment, she alone survived the war. MATHURA steamed on until 1959 when sold to the Harris and Dixon Steamship Co. Ltd. Obviously anagram-lovers, they renamed her THUMARA for her final voyage to Japan and the breakers. *[World Ship Photo Library]*

MARTAND (1) *(back cover, top)*
Workman, Clark and Co. Ltd., Belfast; 1912, 8443gt, 490 feet

Basil Feilden did not date his negatives, but evidence from a similar shot by John McRoberts suggests that MARTAND was photographed on May Day 1937. This twin-screw steamer had a varied career, having run for Port Line and its predecessors as HAWKES BAY and PORT NAPIER. Transferred to Brocklebanks in 1936, she became the Italian MAR BIANCO two years later. On the capitulation of Italy in 1943 the German Navy took possession, and she was sunk by Allied aircraft at Zadar, Yugoslavia in December of that year.

MATURATA *(back cover, bottom)*
William Hamilton and Co. Ltd., Port Glasgow; 1955, 7365gt, 472 feet

Second of the MASKELIYA-class, MATURATA is seen getting up speed as she leaves the Manchester Ship Canal. Like other turbine steamers, she had a disappointingly short career. Sale in 1969 saw her pass quickly from owner to owner, becoming the Maldive-owned MALDIVE EXPLORER, the Ceylonese LANKA SINNA, the Panamanian OCEAN TRUST and the Thai APAI SAMUT, all in the three years before she was broken up in Taiwan.

Also in this series:
Ships in Focus: ELLERMAN LINES
by John Clarkson and Roy Fenton

Illustrating eight decades of cargo and passenger liners, this 72-page book shows how the fleet of Ellerman Lines developed from its foundation in 1902 until it lost its independence in the 1980s.

Available at £9.50 plus £1.00 postage (U.K.) and £2.00 (elsewhere) from: John and Marion Clarkson, 18 Franklands, Longton, Preston PR4 5PD, U.K.